SURVIVING THE PARENTAL STORM

CARIS PETERS

Copyright © 2016 Caris Peters

All rights reserved.

ISBN:1530595584
ISBN-13:9781530595587

DEDICATION

This book is dedicated to my beautiful daughter who has been told for many years that she is worthless. She is so not! She is precious beyond measure, as are all the other women, both young and old that get trapped in domestic abuse.

It is also dedicated to my amazing mum who has shown great love, courage and strength as we have walked this painful path together.

CONTENTS

	Introduction	i
1	Surviving The Parental Storm	Pg 10
2	Finding Truth In A World of Lies	Pg 18
3	The Big Question With Only Three Letters - 'Why?'	Pg 27
4	The Raging Storm	Pg 35
5	Guardian Angels	Pg 52
6	Family Scars	Pg 58
7	Confusion Reigns	Pg 65
8	Treasure In The Dark	Pg 80
9	Happy Sad Tears	Pg 85
10	Walking Free In The Hurricane	Pg 90
11	Re-Plotting The Journey	Pg 99

INTRODUCTION

This is my story: a mum watching her baby girl step unwittingly into a journey of domestic abuse, resulting in many years of addiction and co-dependency on her abuser.

My experiences and the subsequent seismic shifts in our family life due to horrific events, very poor and confused choices and a seemingly never ending story, have altered my life forever.

It is not my daughter's story, as that as yet is untold but it is mine - that of a mother watching helplessly on as her daughter suffers repeatedly at the hand of another.

I have had to stand and watch the teenage years and beyond disappear in a cloud of toxic, domestic abuse smoke.

It won't be funny, as you can probably imagine, although I have always found some form of humour helps in any situation. I have most certainly cried more than I have laughed in the last six years but I have managed a smile on many occasions and that always feels good.

It will be as factual as I can make it. Some stories will be embellished and some will not reflect their true horror but they will all be told as I remember them. I hope to try and capture the impact this has had on myself and the wider family and how we have found ways to cope, grow and move forward from the often paralysing situations we found ourselves in.

I am a Christian and right this moment, I can truly say that my faith is everything to me. Over the past six years, that would not have been the case. I cried and cried out to God to hear my prayer but He was resolutely silent.

The parenting journey is not always smooth but there are many families who end up facing a storm of such huge proportions that it threatens to overwhelm them. I wanted to write our story down as I didn't want the experience of the last 6 years to go to waste.

The impact and scale of domestic abuse is shocking and much more needs to be done to bring this traumatic existence for far too many to an end. Outlining this serious issue, however, is not ultimately the purpose of this book. There are many amazing charities who are working tirelessly to break the chains of abuse and there are numerous great resources that can be accessed. They, of course, need more funding and awareness but these charities are making a difference and helping women every single day.

In telling a few people about the desire to write this book, it has been quite astonishing as to how many parents I have met who have faced or are facing severely troubling times with their child. I believe there are many more parents out there who are living a life of pain and conflicting emotions - loving their children deeply and at the same time overwhelmingly hating the choices they have made that cause so much collateral damage and pain beyond anything we could have dreamt happening to the babies we love and the families they are placed in.

If you are shocked to read that statement, then you will not have reached the place where this is a reality in your life but please don't be quick to judge - just be mindful that this is the sad case for many parents who feel they have nowhere to turn to and can find few people, if at all, who truly understand the damaging choices of their children.

So, the reason for writing this book, was for others in these difficult circumstances to hold my hand for comfort and strength, most probably in the early hours of the morning when sleep is an impossibility.

It will then have been a useful retelling of pain in a situation so often beyond words.

CHAPTER 1
SURVIVING THE PARENTAL STORM

I think one of the first things we try and teach our children is not to talk to strangers. When my son was younger we had a book about 'stranger danger' and the constant paraphrase throughout the book, which he loved to repeat at the top of his voice, was *"just say NO."* We read it together often and that particular phrase and the way he used to love engaging with the story has forever been imprinted on my memory.

'Stranger Danger' is a strange and complicated lesson to teach and learn. If we really took it at face value, our children would not make relationships with anyone. Most new people are strangers until we get to know them! We introduce them to unknown nursery teachers and leave them in their care, they are expected to make friends with a host of children who are new to their world, we tentatively reach out to unknown neighbours and so it goes on. I guess what we are really trying to say to them is *'please don't talk to anyone who could potentially harm you.'*

How difficult is that to assess at the outset? From my perspective now, this is a pretty impossible expectation. We just don't know what potentially lurks beneath the surface of a person who can seem so utterly respectable from the outside.

I met a complete stranger on a train once when I was 17, travelling home from Norwich to Crawley. My parents had to relocate during my first year of A-levels and so I regularly made the journey home at the weekends to be with my family. The Gatwick Express was a familiar place – the American guy sat behind me was completely unknown. He tapped me on the shoulder, asked me what music I was listening to on my Walkman as I was singing out loud (yes it was a very long time ago) and we started a conversation. He ended up coming back with me to my parents' house and to this day (30 years later) we are still in touch. He ended up being the leader of a wonderful choir and orchestra but he didn't wear that on a badge as he travelled on the train.

I knew the rules of *'stranger danger'* but in this case, it didn't apply. He never hurt me and only ever wanted for my good but it might have been so different.

In my daughter's case, she also knew the rules and yet, unlike my train encounter, the man she met did hurt her, turned her world upside down and never wished for her good. He was the kind of stranger that every parent wants to explain in minute detail to their child to stay away from.

He is still in touch over 6 years later and now has a permanent connection to our family as the father of my wonderful grandson.

She was 15 when they met and he was 23 but that fact, as you will later read, was a lie.

How do we know if someone will potentially harm us? How do we avoid the serious pitfalls in 'stranger danger'?

Since that fateful journey on my daughter's train, I have started my own journey, which has led me to unknown places. These places have been dark, stormy, scary and unfamiliar. There has been no parent handbook to read and no guide map to get us back on course, just a sense of being lost and disorientated.

As parents of teenagers will know only too well, parenting enters a whole new stratosphere when the hormones really kick in. Teenagers often start 'trying on' different looks and identities and they become very aware of how they differ from their peers. This can result in repeated episodes of distress and conflict with parents.

I had read books about teenagers and could remember my own struggles with things like acne and bodily developments. I certainly experienced mood changes and my poor parents will concur! I guess I sort of knew what was coming with our firstborn but nothing could have prepared us for these turn of events.

During the severely troubled times with my daughter, my work often involved meeting with mums of newborns and toddlers. I loved seeing the wonder and love that exuded from all these little families but I often had times of listening to conversations about the 'stress' of being woken up at 3am, the fact that the little ones wouldn't take their medicine or whether a dislike of peas would result in poor health in later life! As I listened to these tales, my mind would race to our present reality of being woken up night after night at 3am not knowing whether my 'baby' was still alive, with her not taking advice on any level about what would keep her safe and well as far as peas go, I honestly couldn't have cared less whether she ate another little green ball for the rest of her entire life.

Being a mum of 3, I have much empathy for how hard it is

as a new mum or a mum of a 'trying' 2 year old but from the place on my journey right then, the scale of those problems seemed so tiny compared to the ones I was facing, that had grown to proportions beyond my comprehension and most certainly not written about in any manual.

So, alongside the journey into parenting our teenager, which is challenging in its own right, we have had to visit the place called *'watching domestic abuse up close and very, very personal!'*

We didn't ask to go to that place, we never saw it on the horizon of our family's life map and for the longest time, it felt like we were waiting at a deserted station for the train to 'destination hope' or in fact 'anywhere but here' to arrive, going in the opposite direction.

I guess I have known at a cerebral level for many years what the word abuse means, but not having experienced it directly on any account within my 40 plus years in existence, I can honestly say I had no idea what it looked like.

I do now.

It is the most ugly, hideous thing!

Recently I read an article in a glossy magazine about celebrities abused by their partners. Before being swept up in this scary parenting storm, I would have skimmed over the words, not really knowing what they meant but now I can relate in depth to the stories. However, I didn't really read the page. I just stared blankly absorbing the text as I knew it would say the same thing as other similar articles………….. over and over and over again.

That is the nature of this place – constant repetition. The story is always the same once you get behind the detail – a cycle of horrible violence, coercion and exertion of power and control.

The UK government's definition of domestic violence is:

'any incident or pattern of incidents of controlling, coercive, threatening behaviour, violence or abuse between those aged 16 or over who are, or have been, intimate partners or family members regardless of gender or sexuality. The abuse can encompass, but is not limited to psychological, physical, sexual, financial and emotional abuse.'

We recently got a new car and it seemed as if the world and his wife were then driving the same model as ours - a car that I had not noticed before. It was the same with our situation. Once we came to understand a little of what was unfolding before our eyes, we began to see abuse in its many guises all over the place.

If, like us, you have not noticed this terrible scenario before, here are some recent facts about domestic abuse in England and Wales:

- Each year around 2.1m people suffer some form of domestic abuse - 1.4 million women (8.5% of the population) and 700,000 men (4.5% of the population)
- In 2013-14 the police recorded 887,000 domestic abuse incidents in England and Wales
- 62% of children living with domestic abuse are directly

harmed by the perpetrator of the abuse, in addition to the harm caused by witnessing the abuse of others
- Each year more than 100,000 people in the UK are at high and imminent risk of being murdered or seriously injured as a result of domestic abuse
- Seven women a month are killed by a current or former partner in England and Wales
- Women are much more likely than men to be the victims of high risk or severe domestic abuse: 95% of those going to Multi-Agency-Risk-Assessment-Conference (MARAC) which is a meeting where information is shared on the highest risk domestic abuse cases between representatives of local police, health, child protection, housing practitioners, or accessing an Independent domestic violence advisors (Idva) service, are women
- 130,000 children live in homes where there is high-risk domestic abuse
- On average victims experience 50 incidents of domestic abuse before getting effective help
- On average high-risk victims live with domestic abuse for 2.6 years before getting help
- Most victims – 85% - see on average 5 professionals in the year before they finally get effective support

So going back to just a few months after our beautiful daughter met her stranger, she was now deeply in love with a very abusive man. Her behaviour, her choices, her outlook on life, all changed in what seemed like an instant.

She was so young and had a whole life of promise ahead but she chose something so horribly different. Our parental storm was very quickly raging all around us.

We were drowning.

In fact some days, I think I did drown and was slowly resuscitated back to life.

When my daughter met her stranger on that train and he asked for her phone number, I so wish her younger brother had been with her shouting at the top of his lungs:

> **"Just Say NO"**

I don't know where you are at present as you begin reading this book.

You might be seeing the storm of a really difficult parental situation brewing on the horizon

You might be unsure whether this will be just a heavy downpour (distressing but short-lived)

You might be right in the middle of a storm of gigantic proportions never before recorded or

You might be slowly emerging after the effects of your storm.

It might not be something you are facing yourselves but rather close friends or family. You might be a grandparent, auntie or sibling.

Whatever, wherever you are at, I want you to know right now that you are not alone.

Parents all over the world have and are suffering from the choices and difficulties in the lives of their children. It can be such an isolating and painful place. You will not understand, in many cases, why this is happening to you, as the majority of your current peers with teenagers will be sailing pretty smooth or at most, slightly choppy waters (at least that is what they will admit to).

Please keep going. Our skills and abilities will be tested up to and beyond their limits. We won't get a medal but the race needs to be run because these are our children. We didn't give birth to them and gather up a store of treasured and happy memories to let it all slip away when the going gets beyond tough.

You will doubt yourselves, wonder where you went wrong, question your techniques but please try and give yourself a break…..even just a tiny one.

We are a small but amazing bunch of parents!

CHAPTER 2
FINDING TRUTH IN A WORLD OF LIES

I defy anyone reading this story to say they haven't told a lie. I have – plenty of them – but the older I get, the more I realise how pointless and dangerous lies can be. They can start so very small and yet change into a tsunami of deceit that often threatens to engulf and overwhelm seemingly ordinary situations.

Again, it is one of those parenting lessons we teach our children when they are little. We can often detect, however, when young children tell lies – the chocolate smeared around the mouth that doesn't quite fit with the denial of eating the Easter eggs – the missing pennies from the kitchen table that miraculously add up to the new additions to their purse………..the list could go on and I'm sure you could add many of your own amusing tales here but the point is that we all live in a world of lies from an early age.

However, it's what we do with them, how we learn to negotiate away from telling them and stopping ourselves getting snared beneath them as they swirl around our everyday living, that ultimately matters.

As we entered this unknown world of abuse and our daughter's addictive response to craving acceptance from her abuser, the lies that existed in our family life were fairly simple. They were the kind of ones that were easy to spot, easy to reprimand and correct and easy to not cause great concern in the general myriad of parenting challenges.

Our daughter, aged 15 at this stage of the story, was as far as we could tell a fairly truthful girl. She didn't go out of her way to deceive. She was busy with school and with her great passion in life – football. She had no real reason to lie, as her social life was mainly spent on the pitch and so the party / going out scene was a hindrance to her fitness levels and ability to focus on the sport. It was kicked into the 'long grass' for most of her early teenage years. This was a great relief to us as parents as we watched our firstborn develop and grow into a tall, beautiful young lady with great potential academically and most definitely in the sporting world. We were seriously discussing a scholarship to the States and she was also awarded a place to train at Chelsea Ladies' Football Academy, post GCSE's.

We were aware, however, of her tentative leanings towards the 'bad boys' with her choice of music, her indications of the types of boys she found attractive and other small pointers. As most things in the parenting journey, we felt this would be a phase and as it didn't present any particular problems, it just gently simmered in the background.

We had no idea that a trip out to a shopping mall one non-descript weekend would make the dark side of the world of lies engulf us. The teenage journey she was on at this point screeched to a halt as she met the stranger on her tube train, who told her he was 23. After ensnaring her with some limited romance for a few weeks, he told her he was 27. As our suspicions of this guy grew to huge proportions, we discovered, via his false application for a driving licence that my daughter made on his behalf on our home computer, that he was actually 35!!!

When I use the word engulfed, I hope it portrays to you a sense of being smothered, strangled and unable to breathe. Our beautiful daughter was now so quickly getting swept away in this deluge of lies – his age, his criminal record, his constant change of name…………….big, big lies!!

She also started lying constantly about where she was and what she was up to.

This kind of behaviour, based on my own personal experience and the shared stories of my friends, is fairly standard for teenagers who want to go out and about, getting up to dubious activities without the knowledge of their parents. I was aware that teenagers want to assert themselves more, rebelling against parental control. I didn't face the teenage years with naivety but what we struggled with most, was the speed at which we went from some minor concerns to 'stay awake all night' concerns that involved her living a life of lies with, what was more concerning, a very seasoned and dangerous liar and deceiver.

There was absolutely no way of stopping her and we tried every trick in our parenting book. This world was certainly dark and just when we thought it couldn't get any blacker, it increasingly did.

The journey, for my daughter, has been a cyclical one, and all the subsequent details of this story are based on this world. Experts describe such behaviours as 'The Power and Control' wheel. It is a particularly helpful tool in understanding the overall pattern of abusive and violent behaviours, which are used by an abuser to establish and maintain control over a partner.

A wheel goes round.

Our lives were now spinning with lies, shock, horror, grief, guilt..........a constant swirl of painful emotions!

Our daughter's life was now trapped on the wheel of abuse and lies. That is what abuse is built upon – the biggest lie of all.

> That there is something wrong with YOU

And so there you stay, trying desperately to fix something that was never wrong in the first place. She was now controlled, not by us, or even by her own self but by the abusive nature of her boyfriend. Abuse is totally about control, and we were fast witnessing him:

- Dictating what our daughter should wear.
- Deciding who she could be friends with.
- Stopping her hobbies and other activities.
- Choosing when and what they would do together.
- Randomly checking up on her to ensure she was where she said she was
- Punishing any deviance from set plans
- Isolating her as much as possible from her support networks
- Demanding her limited finances as an expression of how much she loved him.

Parenting at this particular phase of our storm was so incredibly tough. I think we can safely say that we didn't know which way to turn as we circled around each day, not knowing which way up we were. We would disagree constantly on how to handle things. One day my husband would be the tough talker and I would be the soft spot. The next day the roles would be dramatically reversed as we contemplated our individual responses.

People would give us advice that must have ranged across the whole spectrum of parenting ideas. To say we were lost would be a total understatement. We knew we needed to be on the same page to find a way of dealing with the issues we were facing but honestly, sometimes it felt like we weren't even reading the same book. We would argue at the times when we both needed each other the most to try and solve a problem we knew nothing about.

I guess most of all, I wanted my husband to be able to fix it but it was an impossible and unrealistic expectation. He wanted most of all to be able to fix it too and take the pain away, for not only our daughter but for his grief- stricken wife. Again an impossible task which often made him feel worthless. I cried rivers upon rivers and often questioned why his tears didn't flow. They did flow but as many men can probably relate to, they were deep inside. He would go for weeks with showing little outward emotion and then the stomach cramps, the headaches and the painful limbs would emerge as the pain would find a way of seeping out.

We didn't deal with it very well.

We wasted so much energy on blaming each other and not understanding each other's individual responses. It was horrible. We had so little time together that wasn't totally dominated by the situation. We weren't able to ignore the 'elephant in the room' as the saying often goes – that elephant came with us wherever we went and what a massive elephant it was too.

How do you start the day, any day, with the realistic potential that, at best your daughter will be seriously belittled and called hideous names, to at worst, that she would be killed? And probably worst of all was that she just didn't know how to stop the wheel or just did not want it to stop and we had nowhere to turn to for ourselves for support.

This was our living reality and we had to find a way through.

The truth to our daughter of who she was had now been totally lost. She was addicted to him. She craved his presence to gain his acceptance. In the space of a few months, she turned down 2 football academy places, attended and left 3 sixth form colleges, left college altogether for a year, lost contact with many friends, attempted suicide 3 times, wore only what he would allow and contacted him every twenty minutes to make sure he was secure in her whereabouts, to name but a few!!

I began to spiral downwards into a state of exhaustion as I would seek to uncover the truth at all times of where she was and what he was doing to her. I became some kind of ninja female Sherlock Holmes. If MI5 are ever recruiting, put them my way!

I needed her to see who she really was. I needed her to know that she was beautiful, amazing, and perfect in our eyes. However, we couldn't get her to see the truth - she would only believe the lies. We so often were dragged into the lies ourselves, not knowing whether the large bump on the head was really the result of a clumsy liaison with a brick wall or if the red marks around her neck were caused because she found her scarf too itchy.

These were her versions of the truth but they were not true. He physically hurt her on many occasions but as we were never direct witnesses to this fact, we could only look at the cuts, bruises and strangle marks through a veiled cover up of the truth. The emotional abuse was not on direct show, although a swift deterioration in our daughter's mental well-being demonstrated that this too was without bounds.

I'm sure I have had many breakdowns over those years. It started with not being able to plan anything. It was such an effort to get through a day in one piece that it took just too much energy to think about anything beyond going to bed. The panic attacks would come out of nowhere - often after having achieved a fairly minor task such as food shopping. I would have to stop the car on the way home as I couldn't breathe. The physical energy used up in walking the aisles and making food choices suddenly became too much and my body reminded me that it was all a step too far.

I have always been intrigued by a man called Hudson Taylor. I read his story as a young girl and it has stayed with me ever since. Hudson Taylor was born to a Methodist couple who were fascinated with the Far East. They had prayed for their new son, *"Grant that he may work for you in China"* and he did just that as a missionary. He spent many years learning the rudiments of medicine, studying Mandarin, and immersing himself deeper into reading the Bible and prayer. He finally sailed to Shanghai and almost immediately made a radical decision of the day to dress in Chinese clothes and grow a pigtail (as Chinese men did). He worked tirelessly as a missionary in China but it ultimately led him to having a total physical and mental breakdown in 1900. On one particular day he was found repeating the same phrase over and over again: *"You may trust the Lord too little but you can never trust him too much."*

One hundred and ten years later in North London, after I had worked tirelessly for many years to rescue my daughter from the clutches of abuse and was left a physical and emotional mess, I found myself lying in bed, awake for the whole night, repeating the phrase **'Love Wins'** over and over again. I had heard the pastor at my parents' church preach on it a few Sundays previously and it circled around my brain non-stop. That had to be the truth we all had to hold on to.

Love was certainly not what she was experiencing!

The love that I knew of and that had been shared so freely in our family life was so very different to the love our daughter thought she was receiving.

That restless night left me exhausted but in other ways refreshed, as I allowed that truth to seep deep into my soul.

I would find a way to keep going.

I would catch my breath from under the crushing storm, maybe only long enough for a quick gasp of fresh air but it would be enough to help me survive.

I would have to get used to swimming in the deep waters

of pain because this storm was not about to pass any time soon.

Whatever situation you are facing, try and look for moments of truth and clarity. The distress, the lies, the general 'fog' of such destructive decisions by our children, leaves little room for understanding.

I believe it really helped me to grapple with the truth of what was happening but it wasn't easy and it has been a gradual process. It made my brain and my heart ache beyond measure but it gave me a focus and reason to keep going.

I may never fully know why my daughter got so easily trapped in a cycle of severe abuse in the light of the loving, stable upbringing we provided but I know for sure that:

- at all times in her childhood we did our best.

That was true for us and is most probably true for you too

- some decisions and addictions are just too huge to contemplate.

Statistics give a sad but true picture of this fact

- life is filled with unanswered questions.

Most people will say that is true for them or at least someone they know

- we need courage to seek as many answers as possible.

It helps us to stop wallowing in despair, wondering why we were the ones led down this road strewn with unbelievable pain. In this difficult time though, some truths may be not worth knowing. We have finite minds, finite resources and a finite amount of time. What we want to know are truths that matter, truths that are relevant to our practical concerns, truths that will help find a suitable path of action or explanation, or merely to day to day existence.

During those months of endless questions, **LOVE** was my only anchor and true answer - the love of my God and my family.

At that particular moment in time, that would have to be truth enough

CHAPTER 3
THE BIG QUESTION WITH ONLY THREE LETTERS -WHY?

As I write this section, I currently have one teenager and one 'tweenie' living at home and, of course, I have been one myself. I can speak from a small place of experience and for what it's worth, these are my thoughts on how the teenage mind might work in part and how these brain functions have impacted my daughter.

In my own case, I used to want to explore what it was that I would stand for, believe and accept. It was all very well that my parents had taught me many wonderful things but they weren't a culmination of my own decisions - they had somehow became part of me without my permission and I wanted to find my own identity………..

I felt very insecure as a teenager about my looks - being a 'ginger' was a source of endless amusement for many, mostly my two brothers and so I constantly strived to look better by absorbing the latest fashion trend, make-up style and hair-do. As I look back on all the teenage photos, I failed miserably in all areas (the 'perm' has a lot to answer for) and am grateful that I slowly improved with age and that being a red-head somehow became acceptable, if not desirable!!

My daughter did not inherit my looks or my red hair and although and, of course, I would say this as a biased mum she was and is incredibly beautiful; she still had all the insecurities that go with the teenage territory. We started to see our daughter reject much of what we had taught her in terms of morals. She wanted desperately to be her own person but during this time got caught up in believing that her new boyfriend's beliefs and ideas were just the ticket. They made her feel free of the shackles of parental influence but it was tragic to see her fragile teenage brain finding its identity by absorbing the identity of someone else who couldn't have been more removed from what we would have wanted for her as she began the journey into adulthood. He filled the teenage space in her brain completely and she had no room to explore her own ideas.

To have someone specifically ask for her number and an older guy at that, gave her such a boost. She felt like she had won the lottery and her quest to feel beautiful and grown-up rested on that one adrenaline moment.

It became increasingly obvious that it must have been that 'fix' she craved, as he soon began to call her ugly, worthless, a waste of space, disgusting, whore and many more horrible names............ Teens are primed to learn quickly and as addiction is actually a form of learning, they get addicted faster than they would if they were exposed to the same substances or experiences later on in life. She was quickly hooked!

> **These horrible words began to define her.**

It was as if she had to hear them all to be able to get back to that moment when she felt beautiful - that tiny, miniscule moment that was actually an illusion and forgive me for saying it one more time but a big, fat lie.

The reality was that her inner and outer beauty was always there, even in the midst of such ugly talk but she couldn't make sense of it all. Her mind craved that initial acceptance and this seemed to be the only way to get it. It didn't seem to matter that we treated her with love, respect and dignity - we just couldn't recreate that spark which that moment of meeting him on that fateful day gave her.

We tried and we tried and we tried some more to talk words of goodness and love into her increasingly poisonous situation but we could only in the end stand and watch her go round on this never ending wheel of abuse. It was so painful to see my daughter who I loved so deeply being hurt so badly and subsequently basing many years of her life on very poor decisions that would have long lasting consequences. We felt our job as parents was to get her to slow down the relationship and help her think through what was actually happening but even after just a few weeks, it was all too late.

With hindsight, I would have moved to the other side of the world after just a few weeks of my daughter knowing this man, before the addiction had time to fully take root. Unfortunately, the definition of hindsight made that decision impossible, as hindsight is *'the ability to understand, after something has happened, what should have been done or what caused the event'*

We are still trying to understand now what has happened, so making sense of it all back in the beginning was an absolute impossibility. We did, however, make a brave decision to move out of the area when we had a window of opportunity around the children's schooling. It was tough for all of us and we suffered many more months of stress because of it but ultimately, it was the right decision. I felt very strongly at the time that our daughter would be killed if we stayed where we were, with the perpetrator of the abuse just a few minutes away from where we lived. I believe even more so now that we would have faced that utterly dreadful scenario had we not packed up our lives and started on a new path.

The question 'why?' got so utterly worn out in my vocabulary.

My adult mind, just like her teenage one, just couldn't compute what was happening.

I started to research the subject and found that there were very few books or articles written that seemed to align closely with our situation. I guess the closest I found was one written on 'love addiction.' I can't remember exactly how long it took for me to gain some clarity on the addictive nature of my daughter's behaviour but I believe it was about a year into the relationship. I had never heard of the concept before and so I guess my research and quest for the truth, just simply missed asking the right questions.

Over time, I began to understand that the effects of the love rush that she had initially felt, had flooded her body with oxytocin. Oxytocin is highly addictive. Some scientists even describe oxytocin as being more addictive than heroine and the withdrawal symptoms even more severe.

This made me realize that the relationship had an overwhelming pull for my daughter and even though there were numerous break-ups, they lasted only a matter of days before the withdrawal symptoms kicked in and it became more painful to bear those, than it did to return to the abuse.

Although it was difficult to acknowledge, I could see the addiction to the abusive behaviour and it began to make a little more sense, although it still felt like we were living in a fog.

But what was to happen to our daughter?

How was she ever going to be free of this and be able to step off the wheel, if it was as powerful as taking drugs?

It seemed an impossible task but I resolved to love her no matter what. I heard her retell stories I should never have had to hear as a mum and I had to watch her relentlessly craving more of the same, causing chaos and destruction in her wake.

I had to be strong in the face of unbelievable pain, to cry out to God for support and wisdom, to make tough decisions that would try to help her see the reality of her life and to keep loving, no matter how hard. Some days I failed so miserably but the intention to love never wavered.

I think if we sometimes knew the future we are to face, we would give up and run for the hills. If you had told me back then that we would be still living the nightmare six years later, I would have had a heart attack on the spot. The energy for the day would never have been enough to contemplate a further seventy two months and counting, of the pain and distress.

The situations we face are sometimes so tough, it would be

impossible to get our heads around a coping mechanism.

How can we?

I didn't give birth and lovingly parent my baby girl to be addicted to and crushed by abuse but it happened - one day, unexpectedly, suddenly,…..crash, bang, wallop and we were there!

In general, I think life is becoming increasingly difficult for parents with the pressures in our modern society. Many more subjects are now covered in most schools under the PHSE curriculum (Personal, Social and Health Education) Topics such as emotional wellbeing, understanding of diversity and inclusion, looking at gender-based and homophobic prejudice, violence, an understanding of the difference between consenting and exploitative relationships, internet safety, sex, teenage pregnancy, bullying and domestic abuse.

This vital package of knowledge and skills taught to our children and then often reinforced with conversations at home is meant to be the toolkit for coping with real life and they are so very important to discuss but my experience is that it can only take you so far.

There will be situations that just happen beyond our control.

There will be children who operate outside of acceptable boundaries through no fault of our own.

There will be children who completely and utterly break our hearts because they do not make sensible choices designed to keep them safe and to help them achieve a happy, fulfilled, independent and healthy transition to adulthood.

I have known of, directly and indirectly, parents of children who are drug addicts, sex addicts and alcoholics.

I have heard on the news the stories of young kids who go on to murder another precious human being. They too have parents and goodness only knows how their lives must be affected.

There was the recent horrific story of Becky Watts from Bristol being murdered by her step-brother. His mother said in an interview, *"I still love him. I just find it hard looking at the monster he has turned into."*

A mother's love runs very, very deep and it is within our DNA to protect and fight for our children but there are some situations that are just beyond our ability to solve. Recognising that fact and being able to hold the tension between being able to do nothing at all and yet needing to do everything within our power to make it all stop, is absolutely critical for our own survival.

One mother said,

"My first born son struggled with addiction for many years.... We did everything humanly possible to try and help him.... But we failed, he died three years ago.....And we, to this day, don't know what exactly happened. Our family is beyond broken.....Our world is shattered."

Ending up losing a child like this must be so awful. The

fight to keep them alive from the danger of themselves is such a tough path to walk let alone having to face the reality of losing the war.

I honestly don't know if the actions we took in contacting the police on numerous occasions, speaking to the schools, phoning helplines, giving our daughter informative literature, organising counselling sessions for ourselves and our daughter, monitoring her moves where possible to try and be ahead of the 'game' and much, much more, was of any use at all but I know for sure that I couldn't sit back and do nothing.

I could not let another human being repeatedly hurt the child still in my care and for it to be ok.

Not on my watch!

I would talk to her for hours upon hours until I had no breath left. I would write letters to tell her how much we loved her and would help her through. I directed her to websites and materials that would help her understand what was happening. I organized counseling sessions.

I just kept fighting.

Some days I conceded defeat but it was momentary. I knew deep down I had to keep fighting the battle. At that particular time I did not know whether it would change or solve the problems but I had to strive for us all and in particular my eldest daughter, to have a hope and a better future.

No body or no thing should ever take our children away

without a fight.

Keep doing whatever it is you have to do with kindness, determination, creativity, tenacity and most of all LOVE.

CHAPTER 4
THE RAGING STORM

As I have mentioned before, I don't know why you are reading this book.

I can only assume that you are facing or know someone who is experiencing a 'storm' in their life with their children that has no easy answers or obvious ways through.

I desperately looked for help and support during the worst times of our storm but was left with a sense that there was nothing out there specifically for parents. Yes, there were numerous books around the issue of domestic abuse in its various guises but they were written, either by the person themselves, giving valuable insights and help for those experiencing the problem direct, or they were written by professionals explaining the mechanics and science of the issue – again, valuable in their own way but not ever addressing the need to know how to cope and keep going as an observer – a very involved, pain wracked, helpless parent!

I just wanted to hear that someone understood and could help throw a part of the lifeline needed to keep afloat during the storm that so often swallowed us up.

For all of the most intense years of this storm, I went to church.

I was and still am, married to the Minister!

I was numb, cold, and distant from God and quite honestly, church was the last place on earth I wanted to be after a week filled with trauma, tears, questions and no answers. Domestic abuse is relentless and Sunday, traditionally being known as a day of rest, made absolutely no difference to the rhythm of our week.

I went through the motions and acted my part but I just could not feel God's love at this time.

I would sing the words presented to us on any given Sunday but they were just empty words – very little meaning and relevance to my life except when it came to those that mentioned 'storm' of any kind.

There are many such songs but here are a few of the key ones that without fail would cause me to tremble and the tears to freely fall…….

Song 1:

I was sure by now

God You would have reached down

And wiped our tears away

Stepped in and saved the day

But once again, I say "Amen", and it's still raining

As the thunder rolls I barely hear Your whisper through the rain

"I'm with you"

And as Your mercy falls I raise my hands and praise the God who gives And takes away

And I'll praise You in this storm

And I will lift my hands

For You are who You are No matter where I am

And every tear I've cried You hold in Your hand

You never left my side And though my heart is torn

I will praise You in this storm I remember when I stumbled in the wind

You heard my cry to you And you raised me up again

My strength is almost gone How can I carry on

If I can't find You

Song 2:

Faithful one, so unchanging

Ageless one, you're my rock of peace

Lord of all I depend on you

I call out to you, again and again

I call out to you, again and again

You are my rock in times of trouble

You lift me up when I fall down

All through the storm

Your love is, the anchor

My hope is in You alone

Song 3:

Hide me now

Under Your wings

Cover me

Within Your mighty hand

When the oceans rise and thunders roar

I will soar with You above the storm

Father you are King over the flood

I will be still, know You are God

Find rest my soul In Christ alone

Know His power In quietness and trust

I couldn't really sing at all during those pain-wracked Sunday mornings. The runny nose and free flowing tears, whether visible or not, reflected a deep pain. I had to just let the words wash over me. It was impossible to worship when all I wanted to do was run and hide but as the writer of a blog I stumbled across recently quite rightly said, there was something I could do and that something, was not necessarily to sing but to:

> **Keep. Showing. Up.**

Looking back at those ravaged times it was because the imagery, the word, the sentiment of those songs made the most sense.

We were in a storm of huge proportions: thunder, lightning, torrential rain, violent winds, hailstones – the lot.

I kept showing up, not just in church but also in life - I just had to.

The noun for storm describes a

- violent disturbance,
- an uproar.

The verb describes

- to move angrily or forcefully
- to suddenly attack.

Those descriptions described our situation so well.

A violent uproar that angrily attacked our family!

| **Storms can be deadly.** |

The deadliest hailstorm that ever occurred was on April 30th, 1888 where 246 people died in India.

Kampala in Uganda sees the most storms per year – on average 240.

Annually an average 16 million thunderstorms happen across the world!

I'm sure we've all seen one, heard one or been caught in one.

In Venezuela, there is a place that sees more lightning per year than any other storm – it has been called the 'never ending storm'

For most of us, these major storms we experience in our lives appear out of nowhere.

As I write this section, it reminds me of the Great Storm of 1987.

I had a restless night's sleep listening to the howling winds outside my bedroom window but tragically 18 people died!

Earlier in the day, Michael Fish, the weather reporter, told people not to worry. It turned out to be the worst storm to hit England since 1703!

We had many a 'Michael Fish' in our lives, quite innocently

giving their predictions and telling us that *'it was a flash in the pan'*, *'it will blow over,'* and *'it's just normal teenage behaviour.'*

I heard these words coming from really well-meaning people but inside I was screaming:

> *'you just don't understand, this is beyond my understanding of normal, it isn't going to blow over – this has the potential to cause serious damage!*
>
> *My daughter is in love with someone who 24/7 wants to see her hurt and diminished in her mind, body and soul.'*

I'm sure if you are going through the ravages of the storm right now – many people will be telling you it will all be ok when you just gut-wrenchingly know that it won't! It's tough to hear but a little like that infamous weather prediction, it is not done deliberately and is often done to offer help and comfort.

Michael Fish, from what I can make out, it is an extremely nice and well-meaning man!

It helped me enormously to forgive those who said well-meaning but stupid things. How could I expect others to know what to say and do when I didn't even know myself?

I taught myself to 'let it go'………..from the infamous Frozen: *'let it go, let it go………..let the storm rage on – the cold never bothered me anyway'*

We weren't prepared for our storm and actually in reality, we never could have been. You don't start the parenting journey brushing up on techniques to help your daughter when being physically or emotionally abused or to help your son addicted to cocaine or to recite words of wisdom around violent crime. Those kinds of issues happen to other people – people who can 'talk the right language' and have a heads up on the kind of storms they might face because they too have chosen to create similar storms in their own lives or have sadly experienced abuse for themselves.

My husband, my brothers, our Dads – all the men in our lives had never laid a finger on a woman. That particular storm was not part of our childhood, adolescent or adult experiences. We weren't ready with the gear needed to survive. We had some of the 'equipment' in our parenting armour, like love, a moral compass, our faith, family support and these had served us well in the regular downpours of life but to be honest, they just weren't enough to face the

'big one'

We needed more . We needed specialist equipment.

Writing this book now, some years on from the outbreak of the storm, I can confidently say that that equipment needed to survive is all out there but when you don't know what you need and where to get it from, it can lead to many a time being overwhelmed, disorientated and drowning in the downpour.

I am fairly sure that if I asked you the question now-

'what equipment do you need to perform a triple heart bypass?'

-you would be able to guess some of what would be needed, such as a scalpel and a clamp but not all the highly specialised bits of kit that only the experts would know.

That is unless you are a cardiac surgeon reading this book, in which case you should know!

The major storms of life we face as a parent are going to be like that – we will have some things ready in our kit bag but not all and do you know what?...... that is ok, it's quite normal, it's perfectly understandable.

It makes the storm harder to survive but not impossible. It also means that in no way, shape or form have you failed!

It was interesting to find out that the 'never ending storm' in Venezuela is also described as a beacon:

> **'Lighthouse of Maracaibo.'**

It acts a natural lighthouse for local fishermen, who are able to navigate at night without any problem. It has also become a proud symbol for the people of Venezuela – the lightning flash is depicted on the flag and mentioned in the national anthem.

I can identify with that feeling now. Our seemingly never

ending storm has shed light in many areas of my life and out of it has come many good things:

- I have been tested up to and often beyond my human limits and survived. This has taught me a lot about myself.

- I have been able to have many conversations with people in traumatic situations, including abuse and have been able to understand and listen with more empathy than would ever have been possible without this experience

- I know much more about domestic abuse than I would like to but is so necessary in a world filled with this horrible affliction.

- I have experienced a depth of love and care from many people. In the world of darkness we faced every day, it was so helpful to be reminded of the good that is out there.

- Most of all, we have been given the most gorgeous grandson in the world. I call him our treasure, because he is just simply that. Something very precious brought out of a very difficult situation. He has brought healing and love in abundance and I can tell you for sure that is not how I felt the day I found out my daughter was pregnant!

I didn't want the storm, I wasn't ready for the storm, I didn't like being in the storm but we endured the storm.

I hope I can give some insight in this book to help guide you to some of the 'specialist' kit that certainly helped us.

We are emerging – battered, bruised but alive!

PARENTAL STORM SURVIVAL KIT

Being kind to yourself

Just managing to breathe some days is a major achievement! That's excellent so keep going. Tomorrow might mean being able to breathe, smile and sneeze. That deserves an award.

I recently found this quote and I love it. It sums up the first piece of kit perfectly…..

> **On particularly rough days when I'm sure I can't possibly endure, I like to remind myself that my track record for getting through bad days so far is 100% and that's pretty good**

Distraction

Somewhere to retreat, something to marvel, some activity, whether that is a simple coffee, work or a walk in the woods. Something to enjoy that takes us away from the pain, even for just a few moments. Don't let the 2 mix, even if it is for a very, very short time.

I urge you; go find buildings and mountains and oceans to swallow you whole. They will save you, in a way nothing else can.

Christopher Poindexter

Simple pleasures

Chocolate and red wine were mine. They became my friends, a small source of comfort and quite a few extra pounds on my hips!

> **Chocolate Doesn't Ask Questions**
>
> **Chocolate Understands**

> **Keep Calm and Pour The Wine**

A close friend

Someone who can hear it all! There won't be many of those. I had one in particular. She was my 'float' as I struggled for breath in the swirling storms. I couldn't call on her all the time as that would have been too much for her to bear but when I needed her, she was there.

My precious mum was most certainly another – she would listen for hours to just 'tears'. The sound of those tears for her must have been so hard to hear but she listened to my greatest pain.

Never judging. Always kind. Always there.

I needed those two people more than anything. Go find them. Treasure them. They are there.

Dear Best Friend:

I honestly don't know what I would have done without you

Trying to make life bigger than the problem

I have found this to be a gradual journey. The problem was so huge for such a long time that it rubbed against every surface of life apart from the few snatched moments when I was able to detach. Much of the time was pure survival mode but when I became able to lift my head a little, I began to see that I had a wonderful husband, other beautiful children, family and friends, new adventures and experiences to live for. They were worth it. I needed to make space for them.

Enjoy Life Today

Yesterday is gone

Tomorrow may never come

My faith

It was always there but it had shifted to a different place that I wasn't used to inhabiting. Questions, doubt, pain have become an integral part of my faith now. I am still on that journey but I am learning new things about myself and the God I serve. My faith has been fully challenged.

I so wish I had read the book 'God on Mute; by Pete Greig, a little earlier on in my journey as it is an excellent, honest account of getting through the trials of life when prayer seems unanswered. However, I have thankfully read it now and can pass it on as a resource.

Always believe in God.

Because there are some questions even GOOGLE

can't answer

Knowledge and Information

If you are anything like me, you will have days when it is hard to remember your own name let alone understand the issues you are facing. However, it has helped me enormously to research, to read, to talk with others about the issues of domestic abuse and the compounded issue of addiction to it. I didn't start that educational journey until I was in my early forties. I am still learning because I want to not only understand more about our storm but to change the world, one raindrop at a time!

"Education is the most powerful weapon which you can use to change the world."

Nelson Mandela

CHAPTER 5
GUARDIAN ANGELS

I have met a few of these over the last few years.

Sometimes as I reflect on the many events that we have experienced, I suddenly realise that we have met yet another one. They might not be 'real' guardian angels in the truest sense of the word but they were people that were just where they needed to be, at just the right time with just the right help.

According to Saint Jerome, a Catholic priest, confessor, theologian and historian and best known for his translation of most of the Bible into Latin,

> *"each one has from his/her birth an angel commissioned to guard it."*

The Bible is full of references to angels. Angels are mentioned at least 108 times in the Old Testament and 165 times in the New Testament.

I don't intend for this to be a theological debate about angels but here is a brief summary of my experiences and how they impacted me. Even more so, looking back, how they were a source of strength and comfort on the journey in often a very 'supernatural' way, beyond my own design and control.

Angel 1

I received a private message one day through facebook from a lady I had never met before. She had met my daughter on the pavement in North London where she was being dragged by her beautiful long hair out of a car by her 'boyfriend'. My daughter was very distressed – she comforted her and made sure she was ok. She then took note of her name and maybe in the course of the conversation she ascertained a few other details. She took the time to search for me on social media a few days later to say that our daughter had asked that we weren't contacted but she was so concerned, she wanted us to know. She then went on to tell me that she would go to the store where our daughter was working on a regular basis to just make sure she was ok and have a quick chat. I have never met her but my heart knows that she acted with a mother's love and took care of this fragile little girl the best she knew how. I will be forever grateful.

Angel 2, 3, 4 and 5

I had a wonderful childhood friend who I was and still am, very fond of. He moved away to South Africa with his lovely wife many years ago and the times we have been able to meet up since then have been very few and far between. I called him one day in total desperation. We felt we needed to get our daughter away from London for her own safety after being brutally hospitalised by her 'boyfriend.'

Because of the bond we had forged so many years ago, I

felt confident enough to phone him up and ask him to take my daughter at such very short notice i.e. immediately. He told me that just 10 minutes before I had phoned he had met with a couple who felt called into foster caring for 'troubled teenagers.' Neither of us could quite believe it! So, 4 guardian angels in one hit! The couple I knew well hosted our daughter for a week when she arrived and a couple I had not yet met hosted her for a further five. We ended up flying to SA in the final week of her stay, as due to the power of the internet, the abuse had continued and the foster couple felt we needed to be there urgently. It was a privilege to meet them for our 4 day trip and to see first-hand the love and care they showed to her and to us. They gave us a car and in the middle of such a mess we went on Safari and stroked a baby lion! I will be forever grateful

Angel 6

I had to accompany my daughter to a psychiatric assessment at our local hospital to see what support would be required when the baby was born to keep her and the little one safe. She was 8 months pregnant. She was angry with me for contacting the midwives a few days earlier after she had been suicidal and the abuse was pouring like a torrent into her life. She didn't want to speak to them – she couldn't see the point! The storm at this point was raging all around us. I sat with her in the waiting room – she then went in and I was told it would be about an hour. I began to make my way down the corridor for a coffee feeling a little dazed but not outwardly crying. A lady came over to me and said, *"I hope you don't mind me saying but I really feel like you need someone to talk to and I'm here if you need me."*

I work in the NHS and I know that as much as people

would like to, they just don't have much time to freely give to others, other than their patients. This wonderful lady made me a cup of tea and found us a small room to sit in. I told her briefly why I was there and she just gave me words of love and encouragement. I shed some tears, she wished me all the very best for the days ahead. I managed to get to the canteen and buy a latte before returning slightly refreshed and ready to face the storm again. My facebook post that day 26/03/13 said,

> *"God really does put angels along our path – we may not always see it at the time but when we do – WOW!"*

I'm so glad I captured that reference to her. I don't know her name, I have never seen her since but I will be forever grateful.

<u>Angel 7</u>

My younger brother is 12 years my junior. I have many memories of his childhood but one in particular ended up helping me at a great time of need. Many years ago, I went to help out at my brother's 7th birthday party which was held in the local swimming pool. I spent several hours being a safety net for the little boys jumping into the deep end, trying to impress their friends with their enhanced 'doggy style' swimming techniques. One of these young boys grew up to become a lovely young man and to pursue a career in the police. I have met him a few times at family occasions and even though he is now 6ft 3", I always remind him of that time at the party, in his speedos, as a scrawny 6 year old, jumping into my arms in the deep end of the pool.

Fast forward several years and my daughter was severely beaten up by the 'boyfriend' one night and taken to The Royal London Hospital. She was then arrested as the perpetrator had told the police she was trying to kill him (rather than the other way round.) The incident was confusing and traumatic for myself as I watched her being interviewed again by psychiatrists who decided not to admit her as she was 'out of area' and then watching the police handcuff my frightened, abused little girl and take her away for a night in the cells. I pleaded with them to look at his previous criminal record which was extensive and severe but previous convictions could play no part in this current scenario. My daughter, who had not even been in a school playground fight before, was led away bleeding and bruised as the 'criminal'.

My husband and I spent the night in the car outside the police station waiting for news. We went into the police station many times to ask for an update. As I sat in the stark waiting area, I noticed my brother's childhood friend smiling down on me from a Metropolitan police poster as he was the Met 'poster' boy. I know this is tenuous but I felt like my brother and his friend were there watching out for us all. We weren't totally alone in this unknown police station. I remember whispering to the poster 'will this all be alright? I am so out of my depth.' I guess it was his turn to catch me! The poster boy smiled and so we continued with what lay ahead. For my brother, for his great friend, I am forever grateful.

Angel 8

I can only describe this next scenario as like a scene straight from Eastenders. A cockney policeman at one end of our lounge sat each end of the dining room table with my daughter and my husband and I at the other end sat on the sofa like scared rabbits! Our house had been burgled a few days previously with a targeted attack on my possessions and jewellery. We had been away in Devon for a week and the 'boyfriend' knew we were away. The police report landed on this particular inspector's desk and he felt it warranted further investigation as something did not quite add up. He called and heard the story to date of the abuse, the numerous threats to us and our daughter by the 'boyfriend' and he was disturbed to think that our daughter was so embroiled in the situation without fully knowing the extent of the guy's criminal activity and previous record. He came to the house and told us that he wanted us in the room, that we should remain silent and let him speak but that he would pull no punches. He sat opposite our daughter at the dining room table and proceeded to tell her that her 'boyfriend' had a record of being charged with kidnapping, assault, armed robbery to name but a few. He told her that she was worth so much more, that she was a bright, intelligent girl and that she should find the strength to walk away. He said his piece, shook our hands and left. It was a surreal experience as much of what he said was news to us.

This man did not need to take time out of his very busy schedule but he cared enough to do just that. On the outside, his speech seemed to make no difference to the situation but I, for one, will not forget how once again a complete stranger impacted our lives.

My daughter has no idea that I am currently writing this chapter. Today she posted on her facebook page:

> *"Sometimes I meet people and believe they are a genuine angel in disguise. A shining star in an evil world."*

I think those angels will continue to be with us in their various forms.

I hope you begin to recognise some of yours.

CHAPTER 6
FAMILY SCARS

My memory has erased, distorted and confused many events. The events span more than six years now and I can honestly say that for at least three of them, the story of pain and abuse was a torrent almost 24/7. The rest of the years have been a persistent cycle - repeated over and over again with the odd break now and again and by the odd break, I mean for a day or two.

I did sleep in that intense time but it was never for a full night. We would both be awake at 4am every morning. Often I would wake up having been crying in my sleep and lying on a tear soaked pillow. I became physically ill and had to have major surgery. I suffered emotionally and found it difficult to get out of bed every day, knowing that the storm raged on and I had no choice but to face it. My spiritual life was completely non-existent.

I couldn't feel anything around me - it was a very cold and dark place, where looking back now, I know God just sat with me, He came with me wherever I went and waited until I could lift my head high enough to begin to feel His love again.

Our marriage suffered terribly as we were experiencing life in a way that we were unprepared for. We couldn't agree on how to manage our daughter. We argued, we drew apart, we cried, we pretended to the outside world that all was fine but actually it was a daily nightmare. We so wanted to work together but the enormity of the situation simply engulfed us on many occasions. We knew we needed to be on the 'same page' as is often said but seeing as this was a book that we didn't even know existed, it was a tall task and one that we failed at often. What we did find, however, and still do to this day, is that when one of us is strong, the other is weaker and vice versa. This way we can support and encourage each other along the journey.

We also had to deal with the impact of the events whilst juggling a growing teenage son and a little girl who needed her mummy and daddy in ways that we were often not able to give. Our family was torn to shreds but now we have healed or are learning to heal in all the traumatised areas. Yes, the scars are still there and always will be but we have been able to move to a place where the enormity of the events that happened are not all consuming.

We have let back in joy and laughter and that helps - it really helps.

I have several scars on my body. I often joke that I will never be able to get back to bikini modelling but you would have to see me to get the joke!

I counted all the scars specifically for this chapter and I surprised myself!

I have a total of 13.

In the process of counting them, it brought back many memories full of mixed emotions but with great little stories to tell. So here goes in chronological order a very bizarre tale of my scars……..

No.1: the BCG scar on my left upper arm. Apparently I had this as a small baby as I was born in Cyprus and this was the requirement. Good side to this is that I have a great 'where were you born?' response and my parents have many precious memories of their time abroad.

No.2: the obligatory scar under the chin from falling off a bike. I don't remember when or where but I was a little girl. The good side to this little tale is that I obviously learnt to ride a bike, I still have that skill and I have not fallen off a bike since. I might hasten to add that it is a long time since I actually got on one!

No.3: the long thin scar on the inside of my right upper arm. I remember this one clearly. I was still only little, maybe four or five. My daddy had been away on a trip and we went to meet him at the station. I ran to meet him, he lifted me up in his arms, gave me a cuddle and gently let me slide down to the ground………. My arm then started bleeding profusely and a bemused set of parents wondered what one earth had happened. My dad had a short sleeve shirt on with a top pocket, within which was a folded pair of metallic sunglasses. The hinge had caught in my fragile flesh and ripped my arm to pieces. The 3 inch scar is still visible now some forty years later! However, this scar reminds me of how much I was loved as a child and still am. I would still throw myself into the arms of my loving daddy but as my size has greatly increased from my four year old self, I would most definitely cause him an injury instead these days!

No.4: the fairly usual appendix operation scar except mine is exceptionally long as it was done by an inexperienced surgeon and these days would be termed a 'botch-job.' I had the surgery the same day as taking my O-level Home Economics exam which most certainly was not the most ideal combination. I remember the day as if it was yesterday. Crawling around the school kitchens determined to finish my orange and marmalade flan. I did finish and got a surprising 'A' as result. I did, however, lose an appendix and have suffered ever since with subsequent operations due to internal adhesions. It was and has been an on-going problem, so not such a good story except I do remember a very dear friend coming to visit me in hospital who made me laugh so much, I nearly 'split my sides'....quite literally!

No.5: is the scar that is going to prompt a confession! It resulted from a mad evening out at college in Cambridge, with a group of boys who decided to go skinny-dipping in an outdoor pool in winter. It was too good an opportunity to miss to not run off with all the clothes, so my friend and I did just that. However, the escape route involved a climb over a fence which had some barbed wire on the top. As I jumped, the wire connected with my leg and much bleeding resulted as I fled across the field with the clothes. It was funny (at the time) but I now bear constant witness to that night with a long thin scar down the back of my right lower leg.

No.6: The same time frame at college in Cambridge but with a less exciting story. The song 'Lady in Red' by Chris de Burgh was in the charts and as I raced out of my front room to listen to it on the radio, my left little toe and the door frame collided. I broke my toe quite significantly and as time went on, it refused to heal. I went on to have the joint removed and a four inch pin put in its place. The pin has long gone but the scar (and a very odd shaped toe) remains. I still love the song but try to remain seated when it is on!

No.7, No.8 and No.9: 3 scars for the same reason - internal adhesions. Two little ones and one very large one remind me of operations that were quite difficult to recover from. The first was in Cambridge and the second in Oxford. My parents and husband were a great support, as always, and although the scars are there, they have healed, faded and are often forgotten.

No.10 and 11: I have referred earlier in the book to my younger years when I was often teased for the colour of my hair. Added to that, I had 2 large moles on each cheek. My brothers used to say it looked like I had been skewered with a hot poker!! I researched having them removed but the surgeon said it would be too difficult and result in some considerable disfigurement. However, we lived and worked in Cameroon for some years with a plastic surgeon from California. He would regularly comment on how easy it would be to remove them and so I relented and agreed to the surgery. All was going well until the electricity failed and the rest of the operation was carried out by torchlight. As you can probably imagine, I was somewhat scared of the result but I don't think the scars are even noticeable these days. What a story! What a memory! What a fantastic surgeon!

No. 12: now this probably has to be the most memorable scar of all and many of you will be able to share the sentiment. My beautiful third child came into this world via Caesarean section. My second labour was rather traumatic - gorgeous son as a result but a never to be repeated experience. I was so happy to have the opportunity of the elective caesarean that I was out shopping four days later!

No.13: this is my most recent and definitely the worst. My gallbladder was removed in 2011. I went into the surgery hoping that it would be via the keyhole technique but emerged some hours later with a 5 inch scar across my middle and part of my liver missing. It was pretty awful but again it has faded and healed incredibly well. The best bit of all is that I can eat cheese in abundance!

Excuse my ramblings on these scars but it helped me to see that we might face all sorts of trials and tribulations in life but we can heal from them. The memories associated with them will all be different. Some most definitely more difficult than others but there is great hope of recovery.

The scars stay to remind us of what occurred in the past but they don't bind us to it. I started off life with many more body parts than I now have left.

I am missing a toe joint, 2 moles, an appendix, a gallbladder and part of my liver but I am still me!!

I am a changed, adapted, improved version but still myself at the core of it all.

I think this is what happens when we face enormous struggles as a family. We have moments that influence us, shape us, rearrange us and sometimes even break us, just like those scars but they don't have to ultimately define who we are and what we will become.

I am not defined by the number of scars I have. I might have more than most but they have shaped me and misshaped me for the good.

We could not control what was happening in our family life. Our 'normal' family life no longer existed but we had no choice but to keep going.

At times we made a very feeble effort but I believe we always tried to make sure that ultimately love would win out.

Our family was so worth it.

We couldn't give up on our other children, no matter how hard it was to play junior scrabble with our little daughter in one moment, whilst responding to emergency calls about the threat of acid being thrown in the face of our other daughter, at the same time. It was important to do both and that did not come easy.

We were so tired and very little energy was left over to parent two more precious children.

We existed on a very precarious tightrope swaying between being overwhelmed and seeking to overcome. It took a lot of strength but somehow, it is possible to keep going.

Our bodies, just like our wills, have an incredible ability to heal.

I think I am living proof of that but I do hope I get to complete this book before gaining scar number 14!

I wonder what scars you have already gained in your parenting journey?

Some of them will be slowly healing, others may be a gaping wound but:

Healing Will Come

CHAPTER 7
CONFUSION REIGNS

I have searched high and low to find a resource that would help us as parents face this particular trial. It has been a fairly fruitless task, hence one of the main reasons for writing this short book.

I really wanted more than anything at the most difficult times to hear from another understanding mum. I have read online many discussion forums and found the most helpful from a blog written at the end of 2013 in Australia.

The title was:

> "How mothers can support daughters coping with an abusive relationship."

It is a great blog post and captured the essence of the problem for me, with paragraphs such as:

> *"Watching your daughter suffering is painful in the extreme. But don't give up hope. Many women have told me that just one thing that someone said to them months or years before had made the difference to them being able to eventually seek a way out of the relationship! Planting one small seed can make a very big difference. Some seeds take time to sprout. Seeds need the right nourishing conditions. You can be one person who offers those nourishing conditions. For many mothers you have to take care of yourself, have clear boundaries, know your limits, and seek support for yourself. If you have given all you can give and you know you've fully informed your daughter and extended your hand one too many times, you might need a huge dose of self-compassion and to stop providing active support. You have every right*

to step back and leave the door open when your daughter decides for herself to return, and you have every right to close that door if your health is being impacted detrimentally."

There were 98 comments on this post from other mums looking for support and reassurance. Looking back at the other blog topics, this particular one received, by far, the most comments against all the other blog posts that year. I think that tells a story in itself- this kind of resource is much needed.

I urge you to keep looking for help. Your problem may be quite unique or it may be well resourced in terms of support and finding the right help can be invaluable.

I guess I took my lack of support to another level and started to look for answers and find solutions from the services that were supposed to help.

We were offered counseling but after one session, the counsellor had to call the police as what she was hearing was a safeguarding issue of a child under the age of 18. The police came but because our daughter had to make the report herself, we were once again left with no further action taken. We understood why the counsellor had to take that course of action to try and keep our daughter safe but we felt we couldn't trust anyone to help us, as parents, going forward.

We were bounced between the school, social services and the police. Each one had a different set of criteria within which to operate.

- From the school's perspective, we were her parents and had a responsibility for her wellbeing and attendance.
- From the social services perspective, we were not a threat to our daughter so the situation didn't tick that box, our daughter was over 16 so that didn't tick another box and adult services only kicked in at the age of 18 so another box left unticked!!
- From the police's perspective, our reports could not stand alone or indeed hold any weight at all- our daughter at the age of 16 onwards had to be strong enough to report her perpetrator in the face of death threats to her family and herself. Not only was she not capable of that but she needed help with the mess she was in. It wasn't an easy fix and the police could help no further.

Confusion Reigned

In keeping with the storm analogy, I think the feelings we had can be likened to being caught in a 'twister.'

The following are copies of emails that were sent to some key people once we had found the strength to confront the system and look for answers. Apart from the names at the beginning of the email trail, which I believe are a useful context, the other names have been changed to make it less personal. I think they demonstrate an enormous cry for help. I'm afraid the responses were very poor or non-existent and to this day there has not been a satisfactory outcome. It was my way of coping and seeking help.

(my initial email)

Date: Thu, 4 Apr 2013 20:03:34 +0100To: <mayt@parliament.uk>; <libby.blake@haringey.gov.uk>; lynne.featherstone.mp@parliament.uk

Subject: Tackling psychological abuse in teenage girls before it's too late

"Dear Libby, Theresa and Lynne

I have chosen to write an email to all of you as you each have a role to play in my family life and ongoing situation with my teenage daughter, who is now 19 but who has been struggling with a situation of serious psychological and physical abuse from a much older man since the age of 16.

The whole story is far too long for an email but one day I hope you will give the time to listen to the facts of this case to learn from it and to apply any lessons to be learnt in your crucial work going forward.

Today, for me, has brought so many issues we have had with the services across Haringey and beyond (GP, mental health, A&E, social services, police, home office) to a head when my daughter had her 2nd visit from her social worker to our home where she is living. My daughter is now 8 months pregnant and the father is the abuser who has been highlighted to all these services on numerous occasions over the last 3 years. The critical point that I want to raise at this stage is that Julia (the social worker) attended for this visit (the baby is deemed 'at risk' after a further phone call I made to her midwife when I discovered she was self-harming again) with NO prior knowledge of the report that was written by another member of the same 1st response team back in May 2011 where I quote :

"It is clear through speaking with Nicola and her mother that the relationship Nicola is in with John is an abusive and dangerous one. John is verbally, emotionally and physically abusive towards Nicola. He has coerced her into leaving education, friends and family and

pushed her into getting a tattoo of his name to prove that she loves him. She reports that John has slapped her, pushed her down the stairs and throttled her. John has a history of aggressive offences - Kidnapping, weapons, drugs, fail to surrender, theft, handling and criminal damage ......John appears to have the capability of causing significant harm to Nicola and potentially to other young women and I would therefore recommend further action is taken by the police to investigate this matter further."

I believe there is a huge question to answer as to why this would have happened. Julia did come with 11 other police reports and a list of his criminal activities but surely the basis from which to start would have been the information from the initial assessment? This is not personal as Julia was indeed very professional but it highlights a serious failure in the system within social services and as further questions below demonstrate, in the wider care professions and political arena.

These further questions which I hope you will again take the time to answer in full are:

- why have all the services that we have accessed for the same reasons (psychological/physical abuse on a teenage girl) over a period of 3 years not come together and joined the dots? It has always been and still remains a serious picture to complete.
- why have police reports we have made as her parents been incomplete / false in regards to the abuse we fully outlined at the time? We know of 2 such occasions.
- why did the police not take further actions as recommended in the social services report of May 2011?
- why was Nicola not subject to a care plan, when at the age of 17, she is not deemed old enough to vote and yet was held solely responsible for making massive decisions about her life whilst being controlled by an abuser?
- why when I contacted Theresa May by email twice last year about this specific matter, whilst she was leading on the

> *changes to the definition of domestic violence to include psychological abuse and to extend the range to teenagers, did I not even get the courtesy of a reply?*
> *why when Nicola was hospitalised and was completely hysterical, in East London in Dec 2012, after being beaten black and blue by this man did the mental health team say they couldn't "section' her because she was out of their area and they were not sure how the funding would flow?*
> *why when she saw the psychiatrist last week did she not have knowledge of the times that Nicola has been taken to the A&E for trying to slash her wrists and was seen by the same mental health team?*

The accumulation of all the above has resulted now in a pregnancy whereby Nicola has yet again had to prove her 'love' for him by having a child.

Our surname begins with a P and we live in Haringey so please make sure that you do not have another Baby P on your hands. It has all the hallmarks of systematic failure and something needs to be done to address this issue that I know spreads far wider than our own family. Please don't just give it lip service. Help these young vulnerable girls who at the hands of evil, twisted men end up losing so much, if not all of their lives. My husband and I are more than willing to meet with you to go into further detail and help to see whether anything can be done to change the systems that have so severely failed us."

(the first response email)
Dear Ms P

"Thank you for your mail which the Assistant Director has asked me to respond to. You raise a number of genuine concerns in relation to your daughter that this Department are currently in the process of assessing. A Pre Birth Child protection Conference has been convened, which your daughter and family will be invited to — I do hope you will be able to attend. I have been in contact with the Detective Inspector for the Police Community Safety Unit to request a review of the police response regarding the domestic violence allegations. I have also requested that Hearthstone, the Haringey Domestic Violence Support Organisation, also review their response in relation to their involvement with your daughter last year. If we haven't got the service response right we are absolutely committed to understanding why and how to improve and your feedback is valuable to us.

The Domestic Violence Senior Practitioner within the First Response Service has arranged to visit you and your daughter on Monday as part of the ongoing risk assessment. She will also be supporting the social worker in referring this case to the Multi Agency Risk Assessment Conference (MARAC) to ensure a coordinated professional approach to the domestic violence concerns.

I have this morning reviewed the work with the social worker and managers. The social worker will now need to discuss the Initial Assessment and the Child Protection Core Assessment with you. I have asked my Deputy Head of Service and supervising manager to set up a meeting with you and so we will be in touch to arrange this for next week.

I would like to thank you for your correspondence. It is an extremely worrying situation and I, therefore, appreciate your commitment in working with us to ensure your daughter and her unborn baby are protected from further harm."

Yours sincerely
Acting Head of Service

(my response email)

Dear Ms A

"Many thanks for your full and detailed reply. This issue should have been raised some time ago by ourselves but as you may appreciate the stress we have been under as parents in the midst of this sad situation has meant that we have been often paralysed and shocked into inertia, often only having the time and energy to just focus on the day in hand. We have recently felt convinced however that our experiences must not go to waste and be used in whatever way possible to not only continue to try and help our own daughter but also to help those facing similar situations.

Having worked myself extensively across the NHS in senior management roles and more recently with the Care Quality Commission and my husband as a church minister, we know broadly how the systems work but not having had any previous experience of this particular issue, we have been so often shocked and surprised at the lack of joined up thinking and support.

We will of course engage fully with the meeting and look forward to a meeting with the relevant people in due course."

Kind regards
Mr And Mrs P

(my follow up email following an initial meeting with social services)

Dear Ms A

"I am sure N has reported back to you and the relevant people about our meeting last Wed. It was productive in that my husband and I felt we were listened to and the salient points were heard.

We obviously did not come seeking any immediate answers at this stage and I believe it was left that N would feedback and suggest that a wider meeting was held.

I would therefore like to clarify that we will be expecting a meeting where all the reports and feedback from the various organisations is gathered and assimilated.

This process will be invaluable in seeing where the gaps in provision have been and where if possible things can be improved.

Lynne Featherstone has kindly replied to my original email and suggested I meet her in her surgery. I will reply directly to that email but I will be suggesting that it is inefficient to repeat the same story and that attendance at a wider meeting will serve a much greater purpose. Please could you include Lynne in the meeting proposals so that either she can attend or send a representative. I have unfortunately and yet again been ignored by the office of Miss Theresa May. I will need to follow this up separately at some point. It really is a damning reflection on how seriously this has been taken.

On a further note and to add to the future discussion, my daughter contacted Hearthstone last Monday. They were unable to speak to her then and said they would call back. They did not and so she called again on Friday. They asked 'when was the last time he had been physically violent?' and as that has fortunately been a few months ago, they questioned why she had need of the service!! As I hope all of you will agree, psychological abuse is just as dangerous, if not more so, as it *is invisible. I would most certainly say that after she has received a phone call from him again telling her to kill herself a week before her baby is due is indeed abuse and has once again not been dealt with appropriately.*

I look forward to hearing from you in due course with a plan of how a learning review/meeting can be conducted so that necessary improvements can be made."

> **We were never called to a meeting to discuss any changes that could be made.**

The council, however, went on to commission an independent report to look into the issues we raised. The professional commissioned to write the report met with my husband and myself once. The report was issued in draft for comments and it was rife with inaccuracies. It did, however, make it clear that the situation was incredibly serious.

The whole report makes very difficult reading - it is a failure of services throughout. In the conclusion it says:

1. There was a failure to address child protection issues.
2. There was a failure to communicate relevant information about the perpetrator to the child's parents, or indeed to engage with them to protect their child.
3. There was a focus on the child as a young adult rather than a child in need, and when she was a young adult she was seen as having capacity and able to make rational choices, rather than her capacity impaired by her poor mental health.

4. There was no coordinated multi-agency approach, each agency operating independently and failing to communicate.
5. There were delays.
6. There was no strategy to build a case against the perpetrator and no agency interviewed him, apart from the police on the occasion of his only arrest.
7. There was no assertive outreach service to engage with children and young people in this position.

I struggled with this 'failure' but I had to get to a point again in my life, like the advice from well-meaning friends, to just let it go and change direction at that particular point in time.

Several years later and the confusion still remains as to why the systems in place to protect our daughter just did not work. I had to give up the retrospective fight and concentrate on the future. That was where I could try and make a difference. In the here and now!

I have begun to channel my response to this by being a trustee of a small domestic abuse charity and by engaging with the domestic abuse conversation via twitter. The scale of the domestic abuse problem locally and nationally is huge.

It is quite overwhelming but I need to do my bit and as I, once again, gain more strength, I will address the system failures in whatever way possible.

Often when we are in such pain, it is good to look elsewhere to try and make a small difference. It might not be possible for many years to find the energy or the focus needed but it is a therapeutic and useful exercise to try and help others.

Often when children and loved ones die, the family start a charity or harness support for existing ones. It is good to use our experiences in such a way. We have such insight to pain and therefore, being able to relieve that in any way possible for another, is a great response.

Clare's Law was introduced in March 2014. The initiative is named after 36-year-old Clare Wood who was murdered by her ex-boyfriend in 2009. Ms Wood was strangled and set on fire at her home in Salford, Greater Manchester, in February 2009 by George Appleton, who had a record of violence against women.

Her father, Michael Brown, who campaigned for the introduction of Clare's Law, is convinced she would still be alive had she known the full extent of Appleton's previous behaviour.

He said he was "absolutely delighted" that the scheme had come into force.

Mr Brown, a retired prison officer from Batley, West Yorkshire, spearheaded the "right to know" campaign after his daughter's death. He said,

"I must admit it's tinged with a bit of emotion and a bit of sadness but we have got what we were fighting for - to bring protection into the country for half the population,"

Home Secretary Teresa May has worked on a new domestic abuse offence of coercive and controlling behaviour. The law came into effect in November 2015.

The maximum penalty for the new offence will be five years imprisonment and a fine. The new law will help protect victims by outlawing sustained patterns of behaviour that stop short of serious physical violence, but amount to extreme psychological and emotional abuse.

I can only hope Teresa May read my emails, even if she didn't respond.

These laws may not have been in time to protect my daughter but they are here now in our country's statutes and we will hopefully see a much needed change in the way these cases are handled.

I have recently had the privilege of email exchanges with the father of Hollie Gazzard who was so cruelly murdered in 2014 at the age of 20 by an ex-partner.

The Hollie Gazzard Trust (http://holliegazzard.org/) was set up by Hollie's parents, Nick and Mandy, and her sister Chloe. The Trust helps reduce domestic violence through creating and delivering programmes on domestic abuse and promoting healthy relationships to schools and colleges. In addition, it funds hairdressing training for young people who may not otherwise have the funds to study – Hollie was passionate about hairdressing and HGT enables others to follow their dream.

The Hollie Gazzard Trust also campaigns to reduce anti-social behaviour and knife crime. The ultimate aim of the Trust is to positively change the lives of young people through partnerships in communities, as well as working alongside other charities and professional agencies. I would urge you to look at the website and donate some money, no matter how small, to make a difference in the lives they can reach.

This amazing family did not know that they would be working towards these aims a few years ago but they have been unable to ignore the scale of the problem. They want to turn tragedy into something positive, providing a safer future for all, just as Hollie herself would have done.

Our mantra, in whatever form is possible for each individual, needs to be:

You Go Through then You Help Through

The circumstances surrounding this particular storm in our life have most definitely shaped us. We wouldn't be human if they didn't.

My on-going prayer is that we will continue to overcome many of the natural effects and find strength for the day in hand. I thank God when I realise that there are many more days now when we have overcome rather than been overwhelmed.

We are still often anxious but manage to find peace by lifting our heads above the storm

We still grieve what has been lost of our daughter's teenage years and the pain she has suffered but we find comfort in seeing her face the future with bravery and determination.

The weaknesses we suffered in not knowing where to turn

or what to do have been turned to a source of strength as we listen and learn from those around us suffering from domestic abuse.

We might flip-flop between different states of being but I know it is possible to move along the continuum of these feelings into a more positive and happy place.

> **There are no magic answers.**

Doubt, confusion, anger all form part of the process but I hope you feel encouraged that it is possible to leave some, if not all of those feelings behind, most of the time and make a difference to others in some small way.

CHAPTER 8
TREASURE IN THE DARK

The difficulties and pain we faced in life as we watched our daughter struggle were hard. The waves seemed to crash over us in a relentless rhythm that gave us little time to breathe. Often the new wave seemed bigger than the previous one but for me personally, the biggest wave crashed over my life in early September 2012.

Three years in to watching the abuse and emotional torture of my daughter nearly 24/7, I was faced with news that was momentarily just too hard to handle.

Our daughter went to work one evening and sent an innocent sounding text message asking whether we had looked in our bedroom and found her note. I knew immediately what I would find. As I sat on the bed absorbing the eight letter word for what seemed like an eternity, I knew life would never be the same again.

PREGNANT

Of course the simple meaning of that word is that of a

"woman or female animal: having a baby or babies developing inside the body"

But it can also mean

"filled with meaning or emotion because of what is going to happen or be said"

The note sent me spinning. Incoherent words raced around my head. The meaning of the word did not bring happiness and excitement but instead it meant:

| baby abuser grandma future ties panic forever |

I eventually came downstairs to break the news to my husband. My heart hurt so much but my head was numb. It was as if the words that had occupied that space just a few moments before had literally eaten my brain - an image of pac-man comes to mind!

I sobbed. I couldn't think about the full impact of her note. I had a daughter to love and my basic instinct took over. We called her and she came home. The full meaning of the word would unfold slowly before us but in the meantime, I didn't sleep and my head stayed numb for many days.

It was an absolute blessing that something cathartic was just around the corner. I had managed to secure tickets for the Paralympics swimming event for myself and my two girls. I took my numb self-off to Stratford and slowly began to 'feel' again. I watched in awe as the swimmers powered up and down the lanes with maybe only one arm or one leg. It was an amazing, humbling sight and I loved it. I stood up, side by side, with my pregnant daughter and sang the national anthem with absolute gusto.

I didn't feel God with me at that moment or hear him whisper words of comfort but I had witnessed a tangible sense of 'life' and I needed to find a way to survive the wave that had just crashed all around us. It was quite fitting to be sat above the Olympic pool as I resolved to again find a way to keep swimming in the deep waters of our life!

A small verse in the Bible (Isaiah 45:3) reminds me that in all parts of life, God will give me hidden treasures as I seek Him. I wasn't expecting anything that day but I believe God gave me a little surprise to hold onto in the midst of my chaotic heart and numb head and reminded me that He'd got this. I needed it desperately and am incredibly grateful that He loved me enough to tangibly show me.

"And I will give you treasures hidden in the darkness—secret riches. I will do this so you may know that I am the LORD, the God of Israel, the one who calls you by name." Isaiah 45:3

We've probably all read stories about finding buried treasures of gold since we were children. For a couple in Sierra Nevada, this fairy tale of sorts actually came true!

An unidentified couple were walking their dog on their property one day in 2013 when they saw the top of a rusty canister poking out of the ground. The canister contained a bunch of gold discs and they took it home.

After brushing the dirt off of the discs, they were almost perfectly preserved $20 gold coins dating from the 1890s. They hurried back to the location of their first find and discovered a total of eight cans containing 1,427 coins with a face value of $27,980. The discovery was a coin collector's dream: A total of 1,373 were $20 coins, 50 were $10 coins and four were $5 coins. The coins were minted from 1847 to 1894. About a third of the coins were in pristine condition and never circulated in the general public.

It is believed this is the biggest hoard of gold coins ever unearthed in the United States and is valued at $10 million. The couple decided to remain anonymous, fearing treasure hunters would rip up their land.

Finding treasures in the darkness of suffering is more difficult than finding blessings in the abundance of a sunny day, a cool breeze and an easy life. You come across them unexpectedly, unaware of their existence, not imagining that trials and tribulations can yield anything of value. But I believe now, that treasures found in times of difficulty and pain are always of greater value; they are full of meaning; they are not easily forgotten.

In every storm, every trial, every dark day, there are hidden treasures waiting to be unearthed. Our treasure has been worth so much more than $10 million.

The following quote from a lady called Joni Eareckson Tada sums it all up.

By the way if you have don't know who she is, find out! She is amazing and her story impacted me greatly as a teenager. A diving accident in 1967 left Joni Eareckson Tada a quadriplegic in a wheelchair. Today, she is an internationally known mouth artist, a talented vocalist, a radio host, an author of over 50 books and an advocate for disabled persons worldwide.

She has experienced so many dark and difficult days and yet has found treasures along the way. She so beautifully says:

A black night seems to make the moon brighter. Purple irises brighten yellow daffodils. And a dark gray Kansas sky makes the wheat look truly golden. So it is with us. It seems that God best displays the brilliance of His grace against the backdrop of our darkest and even blackest moments."

Our grandson has brought healing, delight and joy into a very dark place. We look forward to spending precious time with him in the years to come, making many memories and smiling at this treasure that shines so brilliantly against our family backdrop.

CHAPTER 9
HAPPY SAD TEARS

I knew I wanted to write this book some time ago now as a support for other parents who are spending their days not knowing which way up they are most of the time, due to serious struggles with their children. I guess I would have been hoping for a happy ending- an inspiring tale to tell, to encourage us all to keep going, knowing it will all be alright in the end but life is not always like that and so this small book reflects the reality of the unknown still to come.

If you have reached the end of your struggles, then that is fantastic but my hunch is that this is a very long journey we are all on.

However, I am learning to accept the massive changes in our lives, to draw strength from the struggles and pain and look forward with a sense of hope and determination.

I still cry often over the loss of my daughter's teenage years and some of the current struggles we face. Those years can never be reclaimed but as is known when dealing with grief, there comes a time of acceptance. The abuse, the damage, the trauma - they have happened. I can't change a thing, no matter how hard I try.

My youngest daughter asked me a short while ago what

would be the one thing I would change about my life if I could. I hesitated for a while as the answer I would have given, without hesitation, a few years ago had now changed into a different response. I could no longer say with absolute conviction that I wished she had not met this man. The treasure that we have found in the darkness would not exist if our daughter hadn't been through this difficult and traumatic time in her life and I truly believe he has been part of the plan to save her from herself. I quite clearly said to my youngest that I wished with all my heart that her sister had not been hurt by this man's actions and words but that we had a reason to look forward and be grateful because of our 'pot of gold.'

It makes my heart break to think of it like this.

Of course I didn't want this experience for my daughter but I had to accept it as part of the fabric of her life and mine. My tears are often a salty cocktail of both sad and happy.

A group of psychologists, who published a report in the journal of Psychological Science, have said that crying tears of joy may well be the body's way of restoring emotional equilibrium.

The psychologists say that, by responding to an overwhelmingly positive emotion with a negative one, people are able to recover better from strong emotions.

The report found that individuals who expressed negative reactions such as crying to positive news were able to moderate their intense emotions more quickly.

The psychologists also claimed that there was some evidence that the reverse was equally true and that strong negative feelings may provoke positive expressions. For example, people often laugh when they are nervous or confronted with a difficult or frightening situation. They cite previous studies where psychologists found some subjects smiled at times of extreme difficulty. I know my mum often laughs in the face of quite serious situations. It can be quite hilarious.

One of the authors, Miss Aragon, said:

"These insights advance our understanding of how people express and control their emotions, which is importantly related to mental and physical health, the quality of relationships with others, and even how well people work together,"

This level of research is all a little too much for me but I do understand it to some degree.

It is so important that we laugh and cry in as much an equal measure as possible for our own mental health.

I have cried a lot less these last few years as opposed to the torrent that flowed in the beginning. I do still cry but much more inwardly. I have been able to develop a more measured, coherent response. I don't understand why this all happened but I understand a little more than at the outset.

This quote is so true:

> **Crying is the only way your eyes speak when your mouth can't explain how things made your heart broken.**

I often say to my husband that there is no real way of explaining what we have all gone through to those who have not been involved. Even then, some of our closest family have absolutely no idea of the scale and enormity of the abuse and its long lasting damage. I often replay the events of the last few years in my head and even I can't believe they happened.

I guess this is why the book was so important to me. For some of you reading this, you will just 'get' the pain. No full explanations needed.

I wanted to be that person for you.

I GET IT!

You don't have to explain. It hurts beyond words to see the child you love suffer so much at the hands of another person or thing or their own disastrous choices.

Abuse, drugs, alcohol, addictions.

They swallow those precious babies up and we have to watch it daily ruin their lives.

It's torture and there are no easy ways through the stormy days.

CHAPTER 10
WALKING FREE IN THE HURRICANE

I have been putting off writing this section for a while. For some time now I have used the phrase to describe the situation we are currently in with our daughter as 'the beginning of the end.'

I am not sure exactly what that means but I face forwards with confidence that she is taking steps to break free to a new life. I have absolutely no idea where this will lead or how long this will take but I do know we will walk with her along this path. The breaking free phase has, of course, not been without major difficulties. There have been more occasions of violence and numerous psychological threats but this is sadly all part of the process. You will find this true of other similar issues as the problem that so easily entangled our children will not easily walk away. There is an ancient phrase which says, *"you may have won the battle but you have not yet won the war."*

There will be many hurdles and obstacles to overcome in recovering and healing from these storms but facing the right direction is an excellent place to start.

I guess this is very fitting for a book such as this as we will all be at differing stages and there is nothing worse than taking advice from someone who has got it 'all together.' I can't give all the answers and there are no trite happy endings. I am sure there are some parents who have experienced deep trauma and come out the other side but my hunch is that the majority of the stories we could share together have a permanence to them that is difficult to acknowledge. I am finding it hard to say that and I am the one writing the book!

However, at this stage in our story, I refuse to give in to any more despair. I want to enjoy the rest of my life. It will be forever tinged with sadness but that's ok. It's a bit like getting on those roller coasters at a theme park day out and really wishing you hadn't. The experience doesn't necessarily mean you can't face the fun of the fair ever again - it just means you avoid the horrific ride in future and maybe stick to the coconut shy (and of course plenty of candy-floss!!) That imagery comes from a place of experience having being forced once onto a ride which left me hanging in mid-air!

I now enjoy the gentler side of life and give me candy-floss any day.

Our storm is still with us.

Some days it rages more than others but basically, I think it is here to stay in some form or another.

We have experienced this as a family. My youngest

was five when it all began. My middle one was twelve. These have not been easy years for them and they have had to adapt, grow and will hopefully move on in their own lives, absorbing the impact as best as possible. They have been amazing and I know will go on to be adults who will serve others and their own future families well due to their difficult experiences.

My husband has been a tower of strength. At times, as I mentioned before, the enormity of the storm out-ran us and we were left somewhat stranded but it was worth facing it together. It has made us stronger. It has given resilience to our marriage that we would have rather not endured but we have and we will continue to enjoy the benefits of it.

There is a well-known story in the Bible where King Nebuchadnezzar throws three men into the furnace due to their disobedience to worship his gold statue. He ordered the furnace to be fired up seven times hotter than usual. He ordered some strong men from the army to tie the three men up by their hands and feet, and throw them into the roaring furnace. Shadrach, Meshach, and Abednego, bound hand and foot, fully dressed from head to toe, were pitched into the roaring fire. Because the king was in such a hurry and the furnace was so hot, flames from the furnace killed the men who carried them to it, while the fire raged around Shadrach, Meshach, and Abednego.

King Nebuchadnezzar, however, jumped up in alarm and said,

"Didn't we throw three men, bound hand and foot, into the fire?"

His men answered,

"That's right, O king,"

"But look!" Nebuchadnezzar said.

"I see four men, walking around freely in the fire, completely unharmed! And the fourth man looks like a son of the gods!"

I heard Arianne Walker, the Director of Mercy UK speak at a conference on this passage. She spoke so clearly about being 'bound' in our fires and storms of life just like those three young men were as they were thrown into the furnace.

That experience was so true for us and no doubt true for anyone else experiencing a storm right now. The situations are often confusing, painful and unexpected and so no wonder we can't move freely at first. The situation most definitely binds us up, makes us squirm and creates all kinds of cuts and bruises from the struggle to escape.

Arianna went on to explain how suddenly in the midst of the furnace, a fourth man appears. He was radiant, even in the midst of the raging glow of the flames. He was God! He unbound the men and they began to walk free in their furnace. They had not escaped the furnace and although the story goes on to say that they were not burned by the flames, it was most certainly hot!! They must have been severely singed around the edges.

I think this is the place we are in right now- walking free, not in the furnace, but in our hurricane.

It is not blowing us away and reducing us to a shivering wreck but it has certainly left us windswept. It is a relief though to walk freely and know we are going to be ok. Our circumstances may not change but we are better prepared and equipped to face the storm.

Mark Twain wrote a short story called 'A Story Without An End.' The last sentence says, *"it is the reader's privilege to determine for himself how the things came out."*

I think that is how this will be left. There are no easy answers, no simple tactics to get our children back on track, no formulaic parenting method to ensure these storms don't occur. We are left to work it all out for ourselves, the best way we know how.

On reflection, I think it is a lot less about what we

can do, although there are many practical steps we can take, but more about what we can get to know, to not only understand our situation but to give us a hope of a better and different future. The degree to which we are willing to embrace the pain of our hurts will ultimately reflect on the process of our healing.

I wasn't scarred outwardly by a rather severe fracture of my elbow when I was 8 years old but the physiotherapy afterwards was excruciating! However, the more I worked at my recovery- in this case moving my arm from a fixed 45 degree angle to something resembling a straight arm, the more I could see results. The physiotherapy exercises would make me cry and I believe my mum had to strongly encourage (bribe) me to attend the appointments, as I knew the pain that was in store at each visit. I have lost a very small degree of movement in that arm but nothing compared to what would have been if I had not persisted with the painful regime. I guess this analogy shows that, the more we are willing to work at our recovery, the better the outcomes.

I do hope, more than anything, that this short book has been a source of encouragement. I have tried to be real and address what I have felt over these last few years. It has been a hard slog and a very painful one but I go back to that small phrase I say so often:

Love Wins

I believe this is still the case, no matter the ending.

We have shown love to our daughter throughout. We haven't shown it perfectly at times of extreme frustration and pain but love for all our children courses through the fabric of who we are and so we continue, no matter how hard our situations become.

I really wish I could just make all the pain stop but I can't.

To have a glimmer of understanding that there is a purpose greater than what we can see in the "now" is a hard truth to process in the midst of terrible pain and suffering but through all the extreme ups and downs of the past few years, I have slowly and gently felt God's everlasting peace and truth on me whilst living in the storm. I cannot even begin to tell you how much I have cried so it will come as no surprise to know that this following story gets me every time!

It's the story of how a man called Joseph Scriven came to write **"What a Friend We Have in Jesus (Everything to God in Prayer.)** Irish born Joseph M. Scriven (1819-1896) was 25 years old, in love and to be married. The day before his wedding his fiancé died in a tragic drowning accident. Heartbroken, Joseph sailed from his homeland to start a new life in Canada. While in Canada working as a teacher, he fell in love again and became engaged to Eliza Roche, a relative of one of his students. Once again, Joseph's hopes and dreams were shattered when Eliza became ill and died before the wedding could take place.

History tells us that his faith in God sustained him. Soon after Eliza's death Joseph began preaching for a Baptist church. He never married, but spent the remainder of his life giving all his time, money and even the clothes off his own back to help the less fortunate and to spread the love and compassion of Jesus wherever he went.

Around the same time that Eliza died, Joseph received word from Ireland that his mother was ill. He could not go to be with her, so he wrote a letter of comfort and enclosed one of his poems entitled 'What a Friend We Have in Jesus.' Many years later a friend was sitting with Joseph, as he was very ill. During this visit, the friend was very impressed when he ran across his poems, including the one he had just written for his mum. As a result of this visit, almost 30 years after his letter of comfort to his mother, Joseph's poems were published in a book called Hymns and Other Verses. Soon thereafter, noted musician Charles C. Converse (1834-1918) put music to that same poem.

After Joseph Scriven's death, the citizens of Port Hope, Ontario, Canada, where he gave so much of himself, erected a monument to his life. The seemingly sad and obscure life of one man resulted in so many lives being uplifted, both in his own time, and for many years after whenever the beautiful and comforting words of 'What a Friend We Have in Jesus' are sung. The words speak for themselves.

What a Friend we have in Jesus, all our sins and griefs to bear!
What a privilege to carry everything to God in prayer!
O what peace we often forfeit, O what needless pain we bear,
All because we do not carry everything to God in prayer.

Have we trials and temptations? Is there trouble anywhere?
We should never be discouraged; take it to the Lord in prayer.
Can we find a friend so faithful who will all our sorrows share?
Jesus knows our every weakness; take it to the Lord in prayer.

Are we weak and heavy laden, cumbered with a load of care?
Precious Saviour, still our refuge, take it to the Lord in prayer.
Do your friends despise, forsake you? Take it to the Lord

in prayer!
In His arms He'll take and shield you; you will find a solace there.

Blessed Saviour, Thou hast promised Thou wilt all our burdens bear
May we ever, Lord, be bringing all to Thee in earnest prayer.
Soon in glory bright unclouded there will be no need for prayer
Rapture, praise and endless worship will be our sweet portion there.

I don't think I will ever have a monument erected in my name like Joseph Scriven, but we do have one in the family, belonging to my great, great grandfather.

It is located in Frome, Somerset.

He didn't know he was a hero, a much loved man who would still be talked about by his family and mentioned in a book 124 years after his death.

The inscription on the monument says:

In Memory of Enos Molden aged 49

Police Sergeant in the Wilts Constabulary, who on the morning on the 12th April 1892, while assisting in the arrest of John Gurd, then charged with and after convicted of the willful murder of Henry Richards of Melksham; was shot dead by the murderer.........

This memorial was erected by the Chief Constable, Superintendents, Officers and Constables of the Wilts Constabulary in recognition of the gallant conduct of their brother officer, who had been 32 years in the Force and was respected by everyone who knew him.

You and I would feel the same about being called modern day heroes but let's be honest; we have, and are enduring very gallant conduct in the face of such difficult times. We are respected and loved by other fellow parents. We have already served, and continue to serve in our roles as mums and dads for many years.

My length of service so far as a mum has been 22 years and I hope and pray for many more to come. We will try to positively impact the lives of others because we know and understand a level of pain not known to all.

My grandson recently called me:

> **'Super Nanny'**

and I wonder whether being able to sound cheerful and smile when all around me has been an utter mess has been my superpower!

I wonder what superpower you can find when all seems totally helpless and hopeless?

> **We are heroes. Superheroes. Plain and simple.**

Keep going for the child that you so desperately love but be mindful that there are others around us who need our love and care and quite possibly the expertise we can share to give knowledge, understanding and hope for that better future.

CHAPTER 11
RE-PLOTTING THE JOURNEY

The famous artist Banksy created a billboard near the Canary Wharf financial district in London in 2011.

It said:

> **SORRY!**
>
> **The lifestyle you ordered is currently out of stock**

All the plans and dreams I might have had covering these last few years have certainly not been forth coming.

I'm not sure what life would have been like had our daughter not met this man. I sometimes daydream and just wonder but not much comes to mind as the reality is, we are where we are. The journey has been different, more problematic and definitely more painful than I would have liked but it is still a journey.

We have not stayed still and today's destination is where it is at!

What is most certainly true is that it has been a journey of discovery. Our new course has revealed many things to us and we have approached them with mixed successes. We know we cannot change the past now and have no idea what the future will bring but the lessons we have learnt will stay rooted and firm within us as we continue to survive the parenting storm.

I hope this story has helped in some small way to support you in your own personal storm. There are no answers as each storm will be different in nature and we will all have differing abilities to cope at any given time.

Here are some of the lessons we have learnt that I am not sure we would have taken on board so fully had we not had to re-plot our journey:

Staying true to our values is really important

We have been tested on this one but ultimately the life we had created as a family with our shared values and faith needed to be strong to bring us through. We both had a myriad of doubts and questions as to why on earth this could happen to us but we needed an anchor to hold us firm. As we move forward, we need to keep them resolutely in focus and take the next steps, not wavering in our firm belief in God, love, family, community and much more good stuff.

Showing unconditional love is complicated

We love our daughter immensely. She was our first baby and we fell head over heels in love with her the moment we saw her. There was nothing she could do to make us love her more or indeed anything to make us love her less. I guess this is why parenting children who cause us so much pain is just the hardest thing to do. I love my husband deeply and he is my best friend but our love, no matter how freely and unconditionally it flows, will have its limits. Our relationship, however, is 'conditional' - we need to act and behave within certain boundaries to get the best out of the unconditional love we feel for each other. The same applies for other relationships we have with friends, siblings etc. I don't think the same applies with our children. The relationship is unique and it would take a situation beyond my understanding to allow that to break. So no matter how much I hated the actions of my daughter at times, the traumatic effects it had on our family and the re-routing of our entire lives, I could not even, for a moment, imagine not being her mum. This tension between loving our child and hating the situation has been an incredibly tough lesson to learn but by going through this pain, I can now live life with my eyes more fully open and my heart more attuned to others who face this mammoth task.

Horrible stuff happens

'Why do bad things happen to good people?'

'It's not fair'

'God's not there' and

'There's no justice,'

are just some of the feelings that have arisen over these past few years.

It has tested my belief in a loving and just universe.

Managing frustration, anger, helplessness, and a whole host of other emotions is par for the course. I have spent many days on my knees weeping and praying for greater guidance and strength. In that place of desperation and despair I have often felt a small sense of peace emerge from deep inside. I have slowly learnt that it helps to shift from whatever we are feeling and thinking to a new way of looking at the issue. Releasing my stranglehold on righteous anger, the sense of my daughter in particular being utterly wronged and ask — what can I do now? Where is there light in these circumstances?

Harold Kushner, a Jewish Rabbi and author of a bestselling book on the problem of evil, 'When Bad Things Happen to Good People' written following the death of his son, Aaron, from the premature aging disease Progeria said,

"All we can do is try to rise beyond the question 'Why did it happen?' and begin to ask the question 'What do I do now that it has happened?"

I can look back now and see that I have gained a renewed sense of faith and am a bit more prepared to ask how this situation can be made better. How can this be a teaching moment? How can I open my heart even wider to encompass the pain and grow from it rather than closing down? And I have also stopped to look for the good that can come out of this bad situation. Where are the blessings? In the end, I believe this is all we can do as we need to come to the realisation that stuff just happens. Sometimes with absolutely no rhyme or reason. We are not to blame.

Life is precious

I so often despair at myself for taking things so very much for granted. I try not to but it seems part of my human condition. I think our storm has made us see life through a slightly different lens. I used to worry intensely about our daughter losing her life to this abusive battle that she was fighting and of course, I still do but I realized I had to spend less time worrying and more time enjoying the good things we had at our disposal. I know it is impossible to live every second in a state of joy and wonder but I know I could do an awful lot more than I do. The struggles of life so often get in the way of the joy to be found in the everyday.

Butter lies unseen within milk. To transform milk into butter we need to churn it. We need to work what is there. I don't know about you but I love butter more than milk so it seems that a bit of 'churning' can lead to better things.

Domestic abuse coming across my path now needs to run scared

I won't walk away and pretend I didn't see. I will take the opportunities on this new journey to look it straight in the face and give it my best, fierce motherly stare and then some, to try and make it stop. This and other destructive and addictive behaviours are an absolute scourge on our society today. According to the Office for National Statistics, 4.9 million women, or 28%, in 2015 have experienced some form of domestic abuse since the age of 16. That is the same numbers as the entire populations of Birmingham, Liverpool, Edinburgh and Newcastle upon Tyne combined!

I will tweet, write, comment, speak out, donate and help wherever possible to highlight the issue and help see changes made to see these numbers reduce. Just one woman, as we know only too well, is one too many.

Breaking the chains and loving our enemies

I do believe we need to exercise forgiveness for all sorts of reasons but for me that will not mean a coffee and cake at Costa any time soon with our daughter's ex-boyfriend. I will, however, love his son (my grandson) with a passion and allow the love and forgiveness that I need to find to flow freely through him.

Again,

Love Wins

I hope, most of all, that now you have held my hand for a very short while, you don't feel so alone and can find the strength needed to face each day ahead, no matter how stormy the weather.

If you would like to get in touch for any further support, please email:

Caris.Peters71@gmail.com

All proceeds from the sale of this book will go to a charity seeking to support those who are affected by domestic abuse.

ABOUT THE AUTHOR

Caris Peters is married to her long-suffering but wonderful husband and together they have three children and a grandson. Caris trained as a diagnostic radiographer and managed the Breast Screening service amongst other interesting and stimulating roles within this profession.

Following a surprise redundancy, Caris set up a strategic management consultancy business and opened an award winning high street shop to further develop her entrepreneurial and business skills.

She is currently working for a large NHS Trust and enjoys supporting and developing the potential of others as they offer their fantastic skills and services to the patients.

Caris' husband is the minister of a Baptist church in the South East and together they enjoy serving the local community in whatever ways possible - mostly involving food!

Printed in Great Britain
by Amazon